Affairs of the Heart
Vol. 2

> "Love's gift
> cannot be given.
> It waits to be accepted."
>
> *- - Rabindranath Tagore*

Affairs of the Heart
Vol. 2

Harlen "Lamb" Lambert

Affairs of the Heart
Copyright ©2017 by Harlen "Lamb" Lambert

All rights reserved. No part of this publication may be reproduced, stored in a retrieval system, or transmitted, in any form or by any means, electronic, mechanical, photocopying, recording, or otherwise, without the prior written permission of the author.

LIBRARY OF CONGRESS REGISTRATION
Lambert, Harlen DeLeon, 1995-
Lamb's Affairs of the Heart: vols. 1-6 ©TXu000718330
Lambert, Harlen DeLeon, 1999-
Lamb's Affairs of the Heart: vols. 7-20 ©TXu000928842

Design and Formatting by
Sharron Read-Lambert

ISBN: 1541042840
ISBN-13: 978-1541042841

Images licensed through Shutterstock, Inc.
All rights reserved to the appropriate copyright holders.
Images appear in no chronological order.

42pix, 578foot, Aboard, alanadesign, Alexandr Shebanov, Allies Interactive, Amir Ridhwan, Andjelka Simic, Andrea Kaulitzki, Androfroll, April 70, Aratta, Arunas Gabalis, Asichka, Bielous Nataliia, Brian Tan, BuketGvozdey, Christine Krahl, Danussa, Dmitry Remesov, DVARG, E.K., Elisabeth Perotin, Eric Gevaert, Fat-fa-tin, Flat Design, Frank Fiedler, Freckle, Gizele, Gori1984, Grygorashchuk Aida, Gulsen Gunel, Helga Pataki, I love photo, Innalnna, japonka, Justaa, Kate Swan, Kevin,Chen, KostanPROFF, Kovalchuk Oleksandr, Kseniya Parkhimchyk, Lauri Barr, LiluDallas, Love the Wind, Lucy Williams, Marina Koven, MarinaDa, Marisha, Mary1507, Nadija 80, nalinn, Nata tata, Nepart, Nonika Star, nuanz, Papkin, ramona Kaulitzki, Sergei Razvodovskij, Silvia Bukovac, Stawek, Svetlana Privezentseva, Svitlana Mazur, Tatyana Okhitina, Telnov Oleksii, Temudzhinova Anna Vladimirovna, Teodata Popovic, Tomo Jesenicnik, Toria, vanias, Vecstock.com, Vlada88, volartman, uso, Yulianka

> "Genuine love involves not only passion, but also commitment and wisdom."
>
> -- *Unknown*

"The heart is a strange
beast and not ruled
by logic."

- - Maria V. Snyder

Table of Contents

THE DAY WILL COME 1
BE TRUTHFUL 2
TRUSTING HEART 4
LIGHT IN MY LIFE 5
TO KNOW EACH OTHER 6
NOT AFRAID TO LOVE 8
YOU DID 9
OTHER HALF 10
OFFERS OF LOVE 11
THE VOICE 12
ALL THINGS POSSIBLE 14
MAYBE UNHAPPY 15
OUR HAPPINESS 16
TODAY SMILES 18
WONDERFUL FEELING 19
DISTANCE MAKES ME SAD 20
FOREVER LOVE 21
ROOM FOR TWO 22
10,000 MILES 24
SUMMER GRASS 25
TOUCH & KISS 26
BEGINNING LOVE 28
SOMETIMES LOVE 29
WALKING AWAY 30
LOVING CARE 31
SOUL MATE 32
SHARE MY DREAMS 34
FUTURE PLANS 35
SO WONDERFUL 36
COMFORT ZONE 38
ALWAYS 39

Table of Contents

THANKS	40
HAYSTACK	42
AS WE	44
ALWAYS LISTEN	45
YES	46
DREAMING ABOUT YOU	48
WHERE DID LOVE GO?	49
FROM THIS DAY ON	50
EVERYDAY BLESSINGS	51
HIS HELP	52
LEAN ON ME	54
CAN'T HIDE LOVE	55
LAST FOREVER	56
A STRONG SHOULDER	58
BE KIND TO EACH OTHER	59
HERE FOR ME	60
LUCKY HEART	61
GOOD NIGHT	62
NO TOMORROW	64
BE HAPPY	65
I CEASED TO LOVE YOU	66
PLACE TO LOVE	68
UNITE OUR HEARTS	69
ANOTHER WAY	70
DOORS	71
A TALKING HEART	72
TIME TO BE	74
DON'T STOP LISTENING	75
I PROMISE	76
MY SHOULDER	78
I'LL NEVER TELL	79

Table of Contents

PROMISE 80

DISTANCE 81

TRAVEL SLOW 82

BONDING 84

IF YOU ONLY KNEW 85

STAND BY ME 86

PROTECT ME NOW 88

ALWAYS HAPPY 89

A PLACE IN MY HEART 90

THINKING OF YOU 91

SOLID AS A ROCK 92

THE SOUND OF LOVE 94

WARM FEELING 95

ONCE AGAIN 96

WITHOUT HESITATION 98

MORE LOVE 99

LIKE NO ONE ELSE 100

FOLLOW YOUR HEART 101

MY MISTAKE 102

MAKE ME LAUGH 104

HOLD ME 105

TAKE TIME OUT 106

THE LONG WAIT 108

KEEP SMILING 109

WONDER WHY 110

MAYBE YES 111

TODAY 112

LET'S CELEBRATE 114

ROAD TO HAPPINESS 115

LOVE AT HOME 116

HAPPY 118

Table of Contents

BE PATIENT 119

PENETRATING WALLS 120

I WON'T BE LONELY 122

YOU WERE THERE 124

BELATED APOLOGY 125

SAY YES.. 126

BE STRONG 128

SAY IT AGAIN.. 129

SOLUTIONS... 130

I WILL ALWAYS.. 131

STAY THE NIGHT... 132

MOST OF ALL.. 134

VIBES 135

A MILLION A DAY 136

SOMETHING TO THINK ABOUT................. 138

JOY TO MY HEART 139

STOOD BY ME... 140

STRONG LOVE.. 141

EXPRESS YOURSELF.................................... 142

DON'T BE AFRAID... 144

DISTANCE BETWEEN US............................. 145

HAPPY TODAY 146

THINK OF 148

THOUGHTFUL... 149

I CAN 150

OUTSIDE WORLD 151

HURT 152

BLOOMING RELATIONSHIP 154

SAD AND LONELY... 155

PERFECTION 156

MY HEART... 158

Table of Contents

DON'T WAKE ME	159
SMILE AGAIN	160
LOVE REQUIRES	161
SECOND CHANCE	162
BEFORE	164
BLESSINGS AND THANKS	165
AIR	166
SOMETIMES	168
TRUST UNITES	169
BROKEN HEART	170
CLASSY LADY	171
I PRAY	172
FALLING IN LOVE	174
AS I GROW OLDER	175
TELL ME THAT	176
REASSURANCE	178
FIREPLACE	179
FAST AND FASTER	180
BEFORE WE MET	181
YOU ARE EVERYTHING	182
LONELY REGRETS	184
HANGING IN	185
LEAVE MY PAST BEHIND	186
MOOD	188
NEXT LEVEL	189
FORGIVENESS	190
FINE WINE	191
WITHOUT MEETING	192
OUR PLANS	194
PRAY FOR CHANGE	195
TAKE A MINUTE	196

Table of Contents

STARLIGHT	198
DON'T JUDGE	199
SHARE YOUR LIFE	200
TRYING TOO HARD	201
BLUNDER	202
YOU ARE	204
WILLING	205
CUDDLES AND KISSES	206
WAITING	208
HAPPINESS	209
TODAY, TOMORROW, FOREVER	210
ENTER MY HEART	211
DON'T PRETEND	212
RESERVED	214
WORDS AREN'T EASY	215
LET'S NOT BLAME	216
APOLOGY	218
DECISIONS	219
GIVE ME THE CHANCE	220
REQUIREMENTS	221
AS I GROW	222
WHO I AM	224
LITTLE SECRETS	225
TELL ME WHAT	226
TO HOLD YOU	228
WITHOUT YOU	229
TOGETHER WE STAND	230
WONDERFUL TOUCH	231
WRONG	232
DISCOVER	234
WHATEVER REASON	235
OUR FUTURE	236

Table of Contents

LET US 238
CLASSY 239
LOVELY THOUGHTS 240
ONE SMILE FOR ME 241
EASY NOW 242
SAD TEARS 244
LOVING YOU 245
MY TIME 246
DESERTED ISLAND 248
STOP AND LISTEN 249
ALWAYS THERE 250
MIRACLES 251
I'LL BE THERE 252
SECOND TIME AROUND 25
EASY TO SAY 255
FORGIVING MISTAKES 256
I CAN'T LOVE YOU 258
YOUR SHADOW 259
IF I CHOOSE 260

The Day Will Come

Every day,
I will give you a piece of my heart
until I have nothing left to give.

That will be the day
I will love you completely.

Be Truthful

Be truthful in our relationship
because it involves my feelings.

Be truthful to our hearts,
because they beat as one.

Being untruthful to your soul
will bring sadness to your eyes.

Be truthful to yourself.
It brings us closer together.

Trusting Heart

I put my trusting heart

in your hands

to show you how much

I love you.

Take care of my heart.

Don't hurt it.

Keep it safe.

Light In My Life

Loving you has always

seemed so right.

I have had that feeling

every day and every night.

Thanks to you for bringing

light into my life.

To Know Each Other

I'm glad for the sensitivity

we share.

I'm glad for the time and

energy we take

getting to know each other.

I love you for sharing.

Not Afraid to Love

I'm not afraid to tell you

that I'm in love with you.

I'm not afraid to commit you

to my thoughts each day.

I'm not afraid to take

our relationship to another level.

I'm not afraid.

Take my heart and love it forever.

You Did

You have fulfilled my every dream
since you came into my life.

I wanted to be loved –
you did.

I wanted someone to share my
thoughts -
you allowed me to do that.

I wanted someone to understand me -
you did.

Thank you for giving me your all.

Other Half

Sometimes I don't understand,
because our relationship is so new.

I really want to be the other
half of a team of two.

I'm willing to learn,
if you're willing to lead.

Listen to the echo in the air.
Is it the sound of love I hear?

Offers Of Love

*I am here to offer you
gifts from my heart:
honesty,
compassion,
sharing,
caring.*

The Voice

On calm days,

the sound of your

sweet and beautiful voice

reminds me of the warm and pleasant

sound of rippling waters.

On unhappy days,

the sound of your

once sweet and beautiful voice

reminds me of the raging waves

of the ocean waters.

All Things Possible

You have made all things possible
since you came into my life:

    friendship,
    sharing secrets,
    love,
    happiness,
    and understanding.

Nothing has meaning to me
without you being a part of my life.

Maybe Unhappy

If you are unhappy
it's because I haven't made
the effort to seek a solution
to your sadness.
Forgive me.
I'll be more considerate,
because I do love you.

Our Happiness

Let's celebrate the connection we have.
I've never been happier
than I've been
since we met and fell in love.
God bless you and our relationship.
Thank you, God,
for our happiness.

Today Smiles

I'm happy today.

I'm surrounded with love and smiles.
Our touching brings warmth.
Our smiles bring joy.
Our feelings make our hearts
beat as one.

I don't have to utter a word
when I look into your eyes.
I see a pretty face
that glows with happiness.
I see peace and contentment
when you look into my eyes.
I want your happiness forever.

I'm happy today.

Wonderful Feeling

Love is not an art.
Love is a wonderful feeling that
comes from the heart.

Love is caring for someone
and sharing it, too,
through good times
and bad times.

Love is knowing how to listen
and to communicate,
saying that I love you.

Distance Makes Me Sad

Night after night,
and day after day,
my thoughts focus
on the distance we are apart,
knowing we have never been
away from one another this long.

The distance makes me sad.

But the thoughts and love
I have for you,
I know what you and I have
can never be tampered with.

Forever Love

I can be there when you need me.

I will be there to make sure
that you are always
protected with my love,
no matter where you are.

I will be there,
because I love you forever, forever.

Room for Two

I see you sitting alone each day.
The bench has room for two.

I wonder – are you lonely?
There are times throughout the day
I ask myself the same question.

I packed a lunch for two.
A lunch to inspire,
as I make my way to sit with you.

Maybe we can meet,
introduce ourselves to each other,
become friends,
perhaps lovers,
and maybe, become as one.

10,000 Miles

Many days and many miles
away in another country,
I found myself
many days and many nights
lonely without being able to
hold and cuddle the most
important person in my life.

I'm smiling and crying.
My heart is beating like a drum.
I'm home.

Summer Grass

From the first time I saw you
I wanted to get to know you.
My mind began to wonder
and to sprout
like the summer grass.
But my heart lay dormant
as it watched
the summer grass grow.

Touch & Kiss

Your lips are so soft
when we touch,
and kiss.
Your arms are so strong
when you caress me.
Hold me forever.

Beginning Love

*Falling in love from the beginning
is like a river trying to flow uphill.*

*Try to think before speaking.
Be kind and considerate.
Communicate until each other understands
what is being said and what should be done
to bring happiness into the relationship.*

*I want to fall in love with you.
I want us to be together as one.
Come to me when you need to talk.
Allow me to protect you and keep you safe.*

*Let's redirect the river flow over time
and fall in love together.*

Sometimes Love

*Sometimes love floats
lazily on the ocean waves.*

*Sometimes love changes
direction as the waves
reverse with the breeze.*

*Allow our love to flow
in the direction of
bringing us happiness.*

Walking Away

Sometimes walking away
has been the easy thing to do.

But walking away
was not always the best thing to do.

Maybe we should think
before we walk away.

Sometimes the hurt
and the scars
are too deep to heal.

Loving Care

Love is like a seed that requires
special care for it to succeed.

It thrives on warmth, time,
and understanding.

Without these elements of caring,
love will turn into weed.

Soul Mate

I can't think of anything but
positive thoughts
since you became a part of my happiness.

Not only are you my friend,
but also you are my soul mate.
We share and compare all of our little
thoughts, never a secret.

Honesty is what we have in our relationship,
never lies.
Openness when we express our feelings of
love toward one another.
Warmth in our arms
when we hold each other,
and fire in our lips when we kiss.

Never a dull moment.

Share My Dreams

I have been lucky to have you
in my life,
filling my thoughts,
and in my dreams.

Lucky enough to win your love.
Smart enough to recognize
the importance of your love.

I have been lucky to have
found someone
so full of cheer,
and someone so dear.

I don't know what I would do,
if I couldn't share your love
in all my dreams.

Future Plans

My feelings are stronger

for you now, than ever before.

It's because of the joy you bring

to my heart,

the happiness you bring

to my life,

and the plans we will make

as one.

So Wonderful

I give you my heart

for the patience

and understanding

you show in our relationship.

You are wonderful.

I love you

for all the things you do.

Comfort Zone

Life is short,
and happy relationships are few.
Maybe we should give some thought
as to why we are so happy and content.

Maybe it's the willingness
to forgive
and the ability
to forget.

Maybe our past encounters
have matured us enough
to allow each other to grow,
and to find comfort in our relationship.

Always

You will always
have a friend.
I will always be there.

Thanks

*Sometimes we forget
to give thanks to
The Heavenly Father
for bringing us together.*

Haystack

Finding love has been like
trying to find a needle in
the proverbial haystack.

Sometimes days and years will pass.
So will loneliness.

Let's kneel and pray to the
Heavenly Father to guide us
on the road to love and happiness.

Thank you, Father,
for hearing my plea.

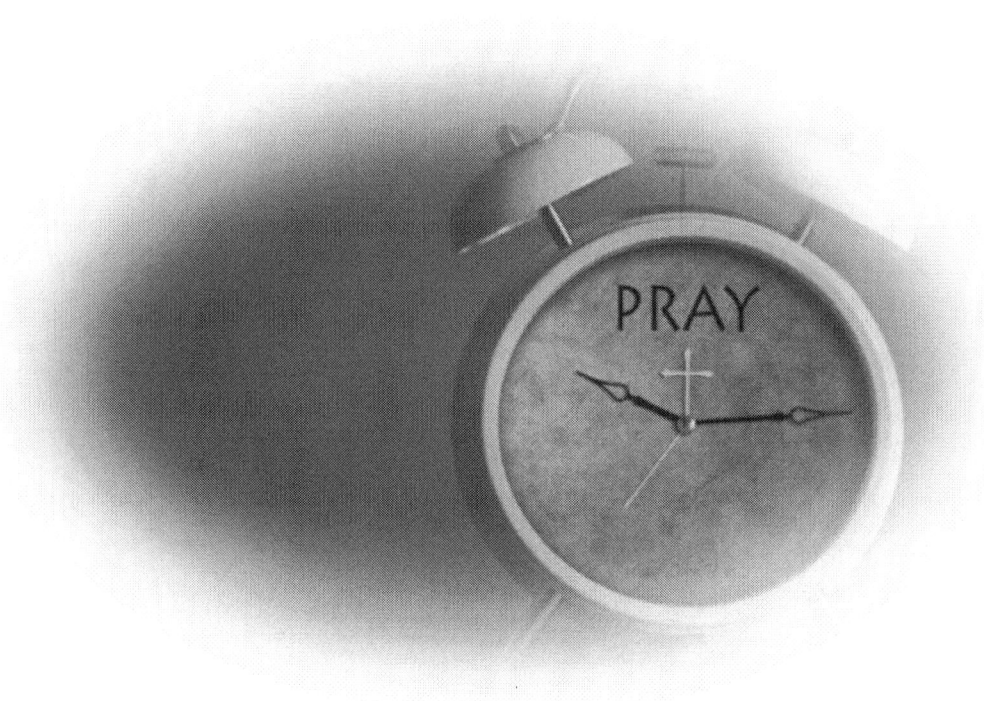

As We

I pray each day for your

safety and the protection

of you and of our relationship.

I pray each day for strength,

as we share our lives.

I pray each day for guidance,

as we try to understand each other.

I pray each day for the energy

to face obstacles from the

outside world.

Always Listen

*Thank you for always
lending an ear
to my sometimes
sadness.*

Yes

*Don't ask anyone but me.
Am I happy?
My answer is -
Yes! Yes! Yes!*

Dreaming About You

I dream about you in my sleep.

*I dream you will share
your thoughts with confidence.*

*I dream you're comfortable,
knowing someone thinks about you
and is willing to love you forever.*

*I dream you know that someone
accepts you for who you are,
and who will protect you
in a time of need.*

*I hope one day my dream
will come true.*

Where Did Love Go?

We are together
as a one-man team.

We just exist,
hurting each other
through neglect
and unkind words.

When did we put aside
our friendship
and feelings of respect?

Where did our love go?

Is it gone forever?

From This Day On

From this day on
I will be there
to enhance your happiness.

To love you,
when you need to be loved.

To be a friend,
just holding your hand
as we walk through the park.

From this day on
you have my heart.

Please don't hurt it.

Everyday Blessings

I count my blessings every day
for my happiness.
It's only because of you.
Thanks to the Heavenly Father
for bringing us together.

His Help

I am someone you can
always call on,
with His help.

We share a close bond and
we've made it through
obstacles on the pathway
to happiness,
with His Help.

Thank the Heavenly Father
for our many blessings,
and His Promise
of love forever.

Lean On Me

You can always lean on me
when you are in trouble.

You can always express your thoughts
when you need me to listen.

You can always confide in me
with your little secrets.

I promise I will always be there
to catch you before you fall.

Can't Hide Love

Love is a powerful word.
For love you pay a price.
It's sometimes bitter
and sometimes sweet.
Love is something
you should never hide.

Last Forever

*Our hearts are now
beating as one.
Our thoughts are going
in the same direction.
May happiness and our future
together last forever.*

A Strong Shoulder

Please share with me all the things
that made you unhappy.
Use my shoulder to cry on.
Use my thoughts of wisdom.

Should you need to be alone for
awhile, I will understand.
I will be here to catch you
before you fall.

I promise a strong shoulder
for comfort
and gentle hands
to wipe away the tears.

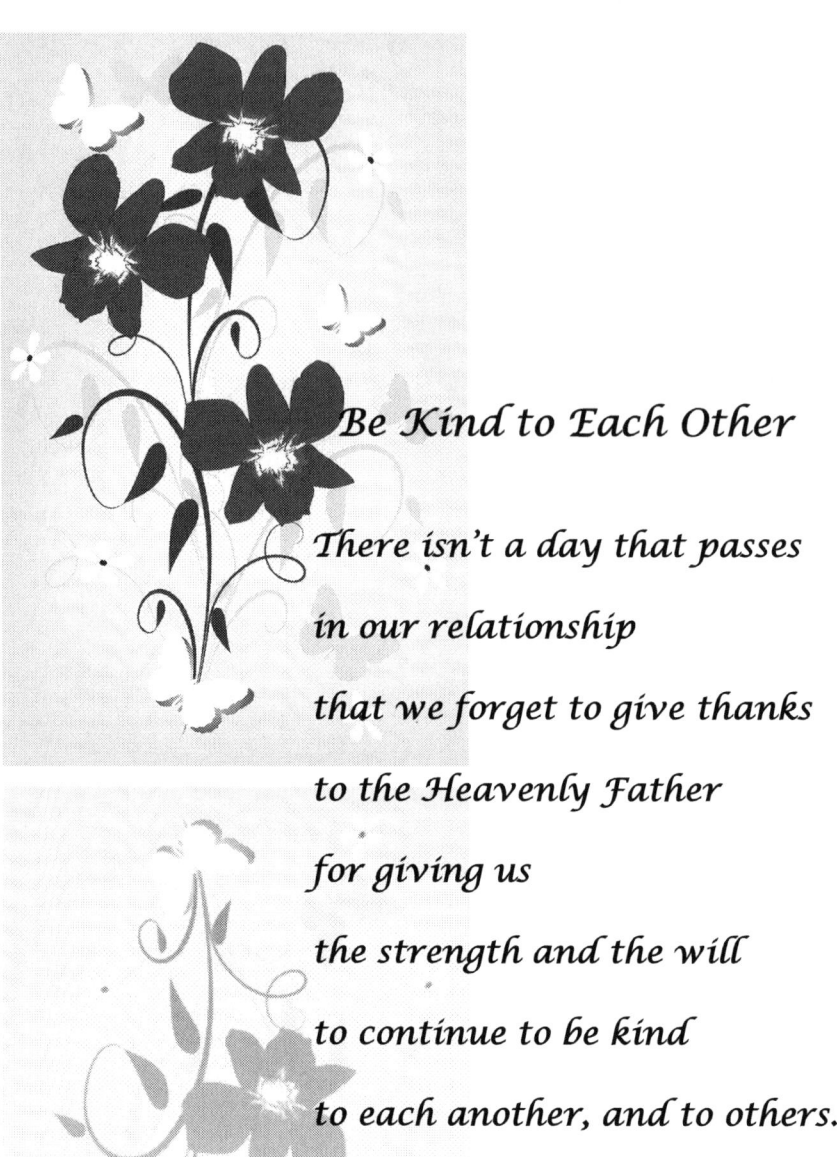

Be Kind to Each Other

There isn't a day that passes

in our relationship

that we forget to give thanks

to the Heavenly Father

for giving us

the strength and the will

to continue to be kind

to each another, and to others.

Here For Me

Be creative today.

Forget about the problems

of yesterday.

Love is in the air.

I feel the breeze.

I feel the warmth

from your body.

I feel love when we touch.

I feel love, just knowing you

are here for me.

Lucky Heart

I have tried many ways to
measure my love for you.

Well, I found that I can't
measure my feelings.

Lucky for you.
You have my heart.

Good Night

*Thank you for giving me attention
when we are together.
Can you remember daily
how many times we tell each other
how happy and content we are?
Especially when making love.*

*Thinking of you when I'm away
makes me feel fuzzy inside.
You are always on my mind.
I can't wait to come home to you,
because I love you,
and look forward to the night.*

No Tomorrow

I'm hoping tomorrow

will never come.

I fear my smile will go away.

My heart will no longer

beat with joy.

I am happy today.

Don't let tomorrow come.

Keep me happy.

Keep the tears away.

This is my request

to the one I love.

Be Happy

*Don't play games
with my head.
Don't play hurt-hurt
with my heart.
Don't be sad,
when I'm sad.
Be the stronger one.
I really want to be happy.
Show me how.*

I Ceased to Love You

I ceased to love you
when I could no longer
think clearly.
I ceased to love you
when I could no longer
enjoy your smile,
your touch,
your warmth and
Your kindness.

Place to Love

I know a place where we must go,

just to find out who we really are.

This place is known as a place

where couples fall in love.

Establish a friendship first.

Learn to communicate with each other.

Find out what our likes and dislikes are.

Learn how to become warm, thoughtful,

kind, and considerate.

And sometimes fall in love.

Unite Our Hearts

Let's unite our hearts
and hear them beat
to the same sound
of happiness.

Another Way

I do not know another
way to prove to you
that I love you,
Other than
by showing you.

Doors

Doors of happiness open.
Doors of happiness close.
To remain happy,
let's keep our doors open.

A Talking Heart

Days are passing as I cry about
something I was accused of doing
many years ago.

Today, the same accusations confront me
and I still deny them.
But where do I go from here?

The day will come,
there will be no more tears.
They will dry up.

Heart - tell me what to do.

Time to Be

Each day I realize how fortunate

I have been

to share my life with you.

You have been a friend.

You have given me

the space to grow,

the time to think,

the time to set priorities,

the time to be who I am today.

Don't Stop Listening

What I like best
about our relationship
is that we listen
to what each other is saying,
and feel it within our hearts.

We express it when we touch.

Please don't stop listening,
or loving me.

I Promise

I will do everything
in my power
not to ever hurt you.

I won't allow anyone to harm you.

I will protect you for the rest of
our lives.

I promise, I promise.

My Shoulder

Go ahead and use my shoulder.
It's always available to you.

You need not fear
you will grow old and lonely,
or that no one cares
about your happiness.

Lean on my shoulder
when you need a friend,
or need to share your thoughts.

Use it to cry on,
and know you are loved.

I'll Never Tell

My friends ask me why

I'm always smiling.

They comment that

I seem to be always happy.

If they only knew.

I'll never tell.

I'll just keep smiling.

Only my heart knows.

Promise

Are you comfortable
in our relationship?
Yes, I'm comfortable with you.

Do you feel what I feel
when we touch?
Yes, when the feelings come
from your heart.

Will you promise to share
your life with me?
Yes, as long as we're happy,
and true to our feelings.

Distance

*Sometimes
it's best if we love each
other from a distance.
Sometimes
being too close causes
unhappiness.*

Travel Slow

If and when you pass through this world,

make it mighty slow.

If you pay attention to everything

people say as you go,

you will always be tired,

and kept in a stew,

because a negative tongue

will always have something to do.

Bonding

Let us walk in the rain,

allow our hearts

to feel the pounding sounds.

Let us walk in the snow,

to allow our love

to keep us warm.

Allow the sun to shine about us

to unite our togetherness

in its warmth.

Commitment and love

have a way of bonding.

If You Only Knew

*If you only knew,
I have been in love with you
since we met.*

*I sometimes wonder
how you feel.
If I only knew.*

Stand By Me

My thoughts are jumbled
since you entered my space.

You've caused my mind
to focus only on you
and the things I want
to do to make you happy.

Just stand by me, okay?

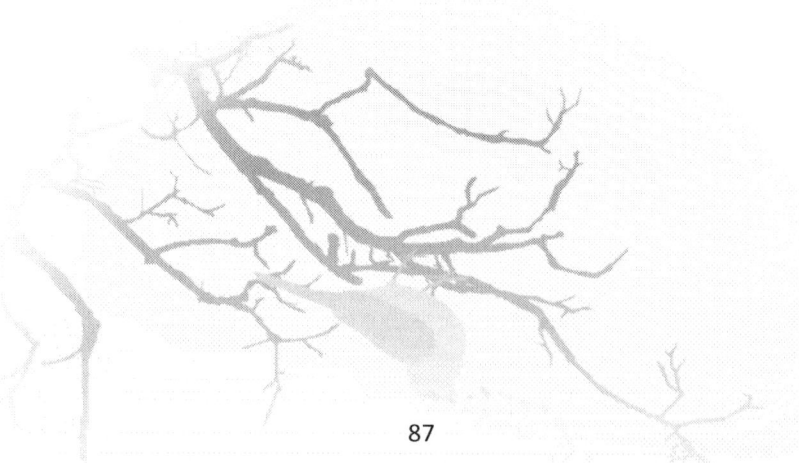

Protect Me Now

We have grown together

like roots on a tree.

As we've grown

our roots have bonded

and intertwined us with

love and happiness.

Our roots have strengthened

us with promises of protecting

us from decay.

Always Happy

Nothing is more important than you being in my life to keep our happiness alive.

Thinking of You

You will never find me *not*
thinking of you.

You will never find me *not*
being responsive to
your thoughts and feelings.

You will always know that
I love you.

Solid as a Rock

Our relationship has been able to
endure many ups and downs.

We have encountered outside
interference from other relationships.

Our continued commitment
to each other to trust, to love,
to share and to communicate
has made our relationship as solid
as a rock.

The Sound of Love

I want to hear the echo in the air
that you love me.

Let me hear it, over and over
that you love me.

I want to hear it in my heart,
that you love me.

I want to hear you
tell the world that you love me.

Darling, I do love you very much.

Warm Feeling

I feel warm inside,
just knowing that you
care about me,
knowing that you
allow me to be
my own person
and to control
my own life.
Continue allowing me
to get that
warm feeling,
because I love you.

Once Again

Tomorrow I'm hoping
to see you smile once again,
as we make changes
in our relationship.
Back to the days
we held hands
and quietly whispered
in each other's ear. . .
I love you.

Without Hesitation

You have certainly made a difference

in my life and in our family's lives.

You have given of yourself

without hesitation.

You have always been thoughtful.

You have sometimes sacrificed yourself

to make our family happy.

I love you for that.

More Love

Can you think of ways I could love you more?

Yes, yes.

More love, I can handle as much as you can give.

Like No One Else

Thanks to you, darling,

for all the years

and times

you have given

to be there

when I needed you.

Follow Your Heart

I gave you my heart,
please don't hurt it.

I gave you all of my thoughts,
handle them with care.

Maybe you could feel the same.
Just follow your heart.

My Mistake

I have been involved in relationships

many times before.

During those relationships

I thought it was love.

When you came into my life

I knew then, those relationships

were only infatuations.

With you, I found true love.

Make Me Laugh

You are so funny sometimes.

You make me laugh, when I am sad.

My heart feels at peace when we touch.

Is it because our minds are focused

in the same direction?

Do you feel the same as I?

Let's walk the same path, laughing

and living happily together.

Hold Me

Hold me.
I need to be held.
Love me.
I need to be loved.
Let me look into your eyes
as I feel your warm body
close to mine.

Take Time Out

Let's not fight any more.
Life is too short.
Could we, for once,
take time out
to communicate,
to solve our differences?
Because we do have problems.

The Long Wait

How long must I wait

before I meet someone who will

become my companion?

Someone to share my loneliness.

Someone who will appreciate my love.

Someone who will catch me before I fall.

Someone whose shoulder I can cry on.

Someone I can protect.

Someone I can love forever.

Keep Smiling

When I see you smile
I can't help but notice
how beautiful
you really are.
Just keep smiling,
because
you brighten up my day.

Wonder Why

*I wonder why my heart
beats so fast
when we are together.
Maybe it's our way of
showing each other
how much we love and
miss one another.*

Maybe Yes

Could it be possible
that I'm happy?
Could it be possible
that I've found
someone to share
my own little secrets?

Yes, maybe I could be in love.

Today

Love has sometimes taken me

on the road of destruction.

Sometimes it has taken me

on the road of regret.

Since we met,

our love has taken me

on the road of happiness.

Today, I don't have the need

for destruction or regret.

Let's Celebrate

Let's celebrate
years and years as a team.

Let's celebrate our happy times,
as well as our rough times.

Today we can openly talk
about unpleasant times.

Our days of uncertainty
have made our relationship stronger.

Let's celebrate today's happiness.

Road of Happiness

Perhaps I require more
than you can give,
or perhaps you give me more
than I require.
Perhaps it's time for us
to discuss and resolve
our requirements,
so we can share the same
road of happiness.

Love At Home

*It's so enjoyable
to come home to you,
to know that I'm loved,
to know that we are sharing
our lives as one.
Thank you for
the love and effort
you bring into
our home of love.*

Happy

Sometimes I find it hard
to contain myself,
because I'm so happy
with you in my life.

You have brought
fulfillment into my world.

Your thoughtfulness towards me
can't be measured in any way.

I love you for all the things
you do to make me happy.

Be Patient

*I beg of you to be patient
with me.
Our relationship is
so young.
Allow it to sprout like
the green meadow.*

Penetrating Walls

I want to understand you
the best I can.
Allow me to penetrate
the wall
that protects you from
the outside world.

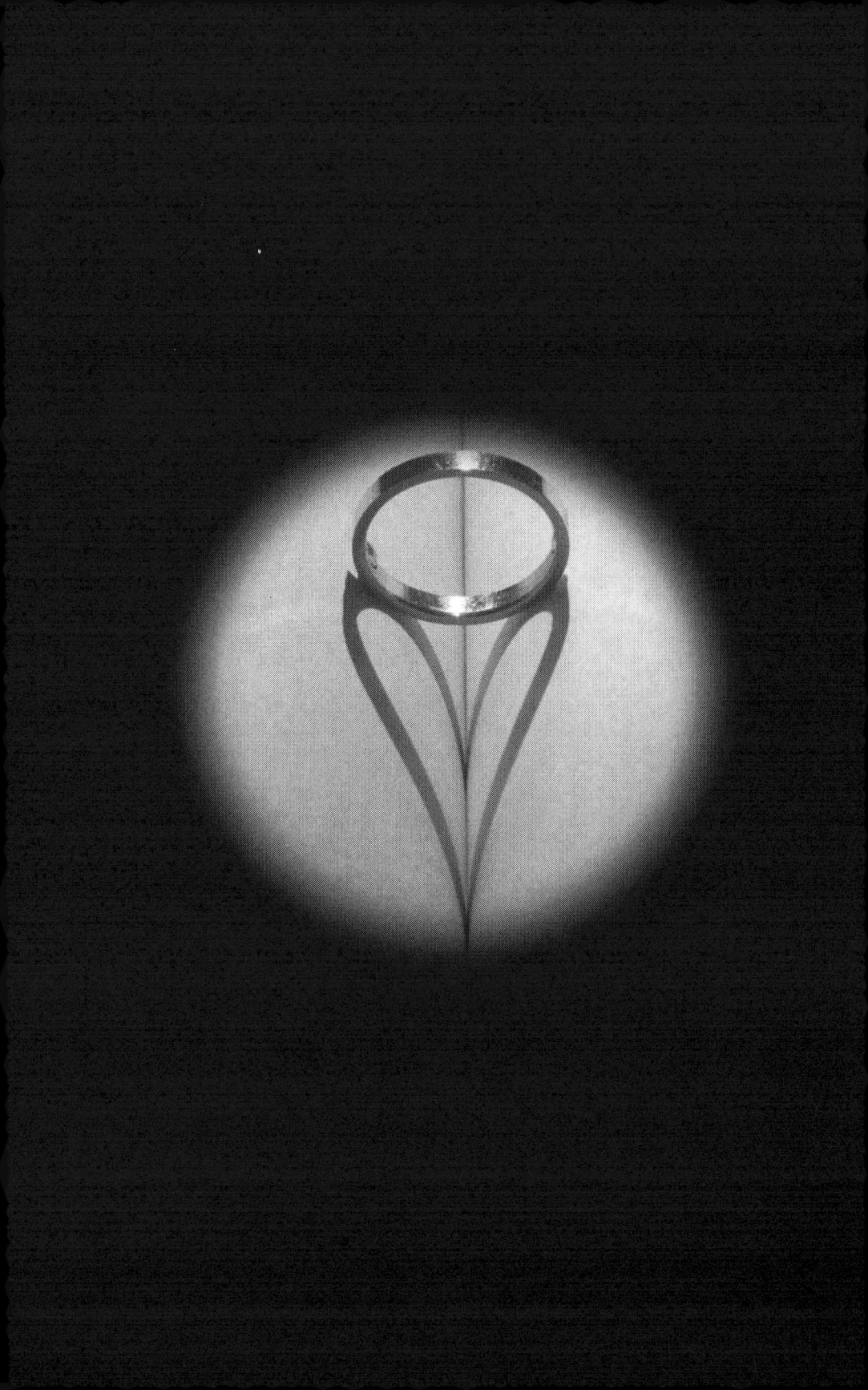

I Won't Be Lonely

Lonely, I will never be

since you came into

my space of unhappiness.

You have brought me

mountains of joy.

Now allow me to show you

how I truly feel.

Will you marry me?

If the answer is yes,

I won't be lonely any more.

You Were There

When I needed to be held,

you were there.

When I needed to share

my thoughts and secrets,

you were there.

When my heart needed

to be reassured,

you were there to listen.

You were there to keep it

and make it yours.

Belated Apology

There are times I should have apologized to the one I love.

Someone who has made me successful.
Someone who caught me before I could fall.
Someone who promised to love and to protect me forever.

Please accept my belated apologies for not always appreciating you.

Say Yes

We are miles and miles apart.

I'm not happy occupying
my empty space.

Perhaps you feel the same.

The day has come,
I'm on my way home
to find you.

Say yes,
share with me
a happy space.

Be Strong

*Can you reassure me that you will
be strong in times of being lonely?*

*Can you be strong
when crying endless tears?*

*My wish has come true.
I have met someone who is willing
to share and be strong
during my unhappy times.*

Say it Again

Say it again.

Say it again,

that you love me.

I love you.

Every time

I hear you say

that you love me,

my heart beats fast,

then faster.

My mind runs wild.

Solutions

Mistakes and misunderstandings are often made in relationships. How can we find solutions before we hurt one another?

I Will Always

Make me yours to keep.

Make me yours to keep forever.

Just in case you forget,
I will be here always.

Stay the Night

Stay with me.

Each day, each night, each week

through the year.

Let me show you that

I'm in love with you.

I'm ready and willing

to share our lives together.

Stay the night,

so I can show you

I am committed to you.

Most of All

Do we really listen

when we talk,

and understand all the things

we are trying to convey

to each other?

Maybe we should stop,

not long,

but just long enough, to listen.

Listen with our minds open,

and most of all,

Listen with our hearts.

Vibes

I can't express or control myself
when you approach my space.

I become speechless
with the vibes you bring.

Sounds like I may be in love!

A Million a Day

Do you know how many times
I tell you I love you each day?
I'm not sure – maybe one million.

I'm sure it's not a million each day.
But I am sure you hear
"I love you" enough to sustain
you throughout the day.

Something to Think About

Perhaps we should focus and work on

the weak points in our relationship:

trust,

respect,

sharing,

commitment,

communication and understanding.

Something to think about!

Joy to My Heart

I trust you with my thoughts,

my own little secrets.

I trust you to bring me happiness.

Just being with you,

I'm always happy.

I trust you when I'm sad.

Only you can bring smiles, and

joy to my heart.

I love you.

Stood By Me

Behind my success

you have been there

for me every step of the way.

I realize there were times

you felt neglected,

but you stood by me.

I'm sorry for the times

you were unhappy

and

for the times you felt left out.

Strong Love

I'm asking you never to doubt
our love for each other.

We have the ability to withstand
outside interference.

Our love is strong.

Only the Heavenly Father
can separate us.

Express Yourself

It's okay if you shed a tear

when you're trying to express

your happiness and love.

It's okay for you not to

be able to express yourself

when you're happy and tears

are flowing from your eyes.

I understand,

because I sometimes try to

hide my feelings and tears.

Don't Be Afraid

Turn down the light
and stay the night.

You don't have to be
afraid any more.

Tonight will be the night
we will share
our love and feelings.

Don't be afraid.

The timing is right.

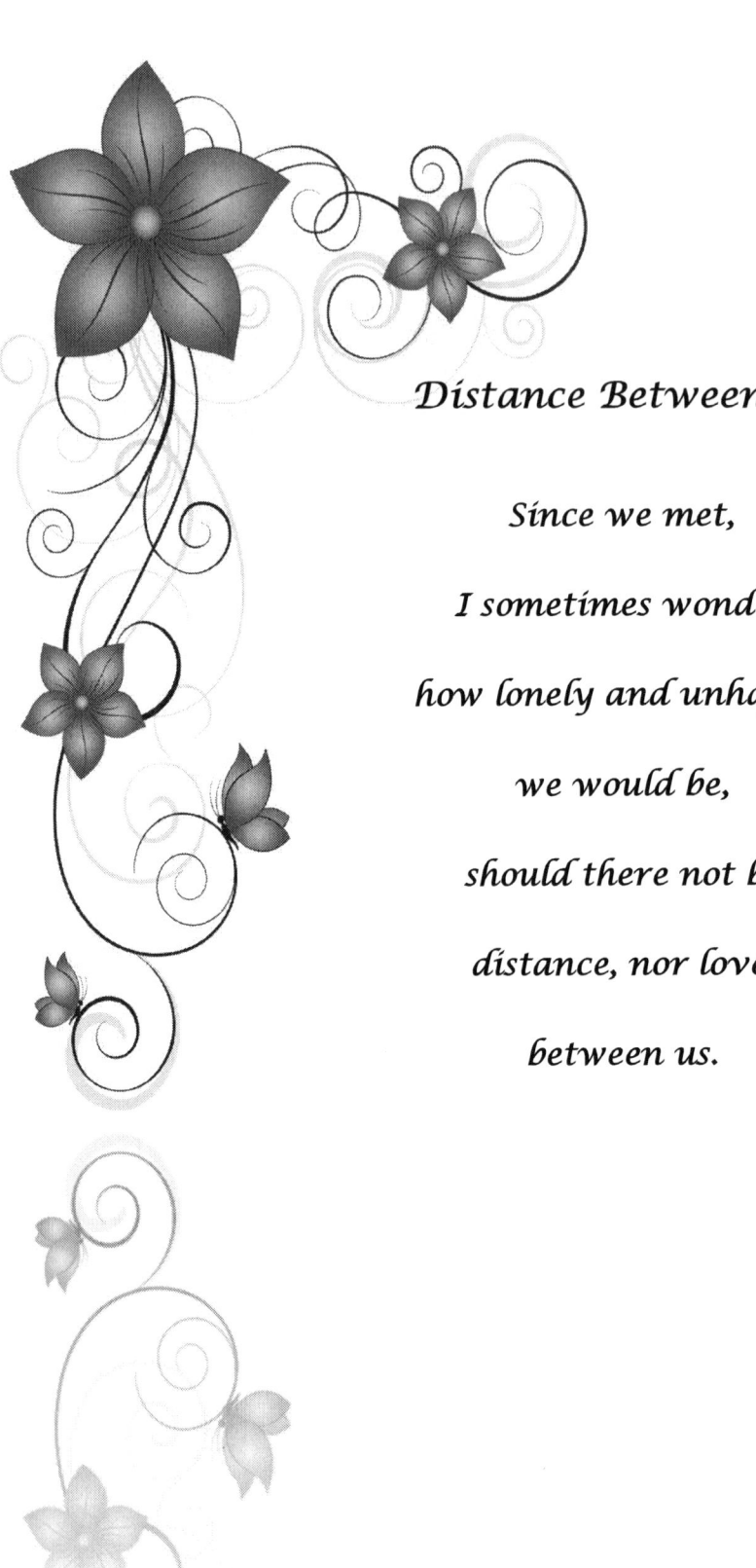

Distance Between Us

Since we met,

I sometimes wonder

how lonely and unhappy

we would be,

should there not be

distance, nor love,

between us.

Happy Today

Yesterday I was sad

because I hurt you,

allowing my past to

affect our present.

I fear what the future

holds between us.

I'm sorry I hurt you.

Forgive me.

Let's try

to be happy today.

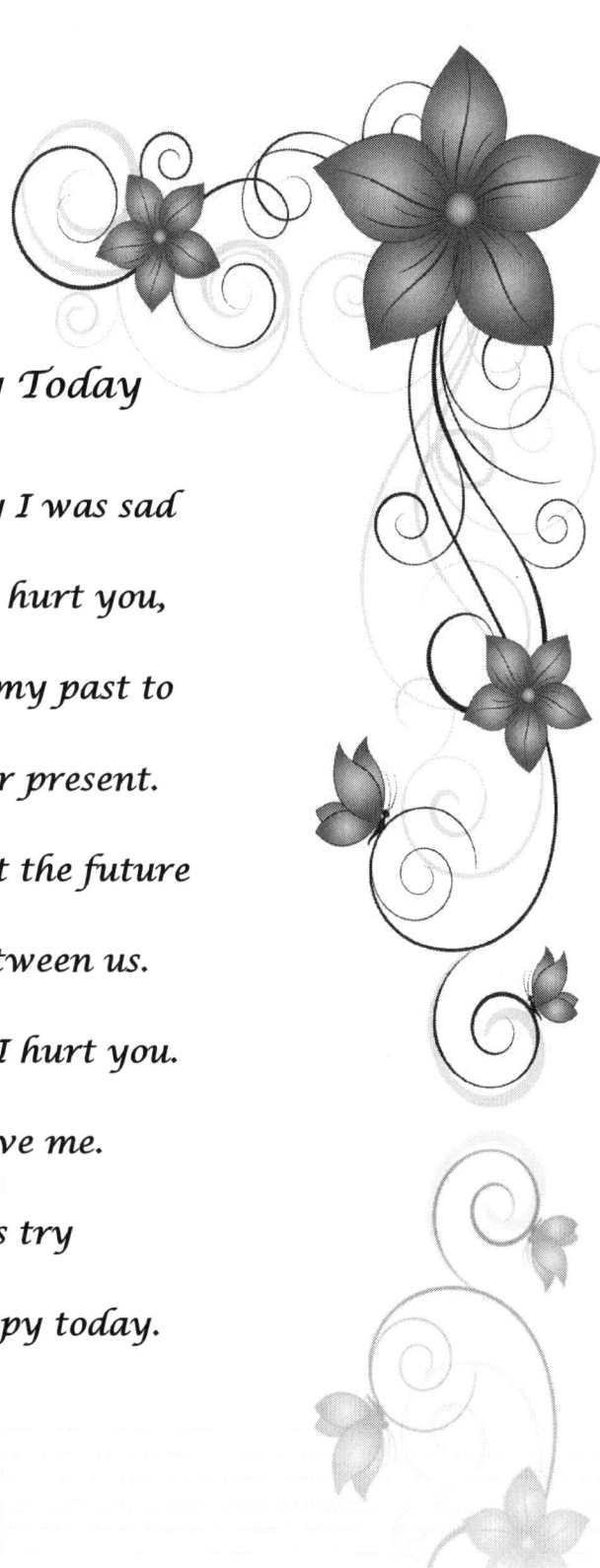

Think Of

When we are not together

I think of the word

distance.

Distance reminds me of the word

space.

Space makes me think of being

apart and lonely.

Perhaps we should be more sensitive

about our distance

and our loneliness.

Thoughtful

I can't think of a time
in our relationship
that you weren't
thoughtful,
kind,
considerate,
willing to share,
and most of all,
tried to make me happy.

I Can

Ask yourself - are you content?
Can you smile about our little secrets?

I can.

Do you hear a little voice
telling you that maybe
you are in love?

I can.

Outside World

As we walk along the beach,
I see your happy smile.
Is it because your heart
feels love?
Or is it because you feel protected
from the outside world?

Hurt

Don't shut me out.

Allow me to be a part of your life.

Don't run.

Allow me to hurt when you hurt,

to be happy when you are.

Allow me to love you,

when you need to be loved.

I love you.

Blooming Relationship

Our relationship has blossomed,

because we've allowed each other

to communicate and to be

sensitive to our feelings.

Let's thank one another for

our flourishing relationship.

Sad and Lonely

I sit alone, lonely,
when we are not together.
I wonder if you
feel my loneliness.
My heart is sad,
because we are apart.

My Heart

Tell me that our love

is strong.

Tell me that our hearts

beat as one.

Tell me that your days

are beautiful and bright

because I am in your life.

Thank you for the happiness

you bring to my heart.

I love you.

Don't Wake Me

When I sleep,

you visit me in my dreams.

Your dream visits are so real

that when I awaken,

I try to fall asleep again.

Please don't wake me

from my sleep.

Smile Again

There were times in my life

I was frightened and confused

because of loneliness.

Today you have filled my life
with happiness.

I'm no longer frightened,

confused or lonely.

I can smile again.

Love Requires

To love
requires effort
and hard work.

Second Chance

I'm so lonely.

I can't bear the thought

of being without you.

Can we communicate

with each other

just long enough for me to say

I'm so sorry for hurting you?

I am worthy

of a second chance.

Before

Before I met you,

I thought I was happy.

Before I met you,

I did not take the time

to learn how to share,

how to feel,

or how to love.

You changed my life.

Blessings and Thanks

*I give thanks to the
Heavenly Father each day.
I ask Him to bless you and keep you safe.*

*I thank Him for giving you the strength
you have in our relationship.*

*Today I'm saying thanks to you
for all the things you do to keep
our relationship together.*

Air

Time is of the essence.

Love is in the air.

Now is the time

to find love.

Sometimes

Sometimes you refuse

to answer my questions.

You seem to stall and maybe

lose your thoughts.

It appears that you can't

give me an answer.

You look frightened and afraid,

and wonder what to say.

Okay – I get it.

But I still love you.

Trust Unites

Genuine love curbs temptation.

Love influences commitment.

Our commitment controls

our happiness.

Our love is strong and

committed to togetherness.

Trust unites our futures.

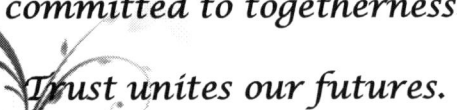

Broken Heart

Our relationship has ended.

I'm sad,

with a broken heart.

I'm trying

to pick up the pieces.

To exist

without your shadow

to protect me.

Classy Lady

Thank you for being the
classy lady you are.
Your smile, your walk,
require attention.
Your mere presence
demands respect.

I Pray

Every time I fall in love,

I fail.

Every time I give my heart away,

I fail.

Every time I try to be happy,

I fail.

Every time I attempt to communicate,

I fail.

I pray for strength and guidance

to help me be happy in our relationship,

and to not fail.

Falling in Love

You don't have to speak,

or utter a sound.

Your smile generates

a tingling feeling

in my little heart,

and big butterflies

in my stomach.

Maybe I'm falling in love.

Maybe I already have.

As I Grow Older

*As I grow older, I will learn
how to love someone
who will accept me as I am.*

*Someone who will teach me
the definition of love.*

*Someone I can love
and accept as they are.*

Tell Me That

*Tell me that you
love me.
Tell me that you
would catch me before a fall.
Tell me that I'm
worth being one with you.
Tell me that our
love is wonderful.*

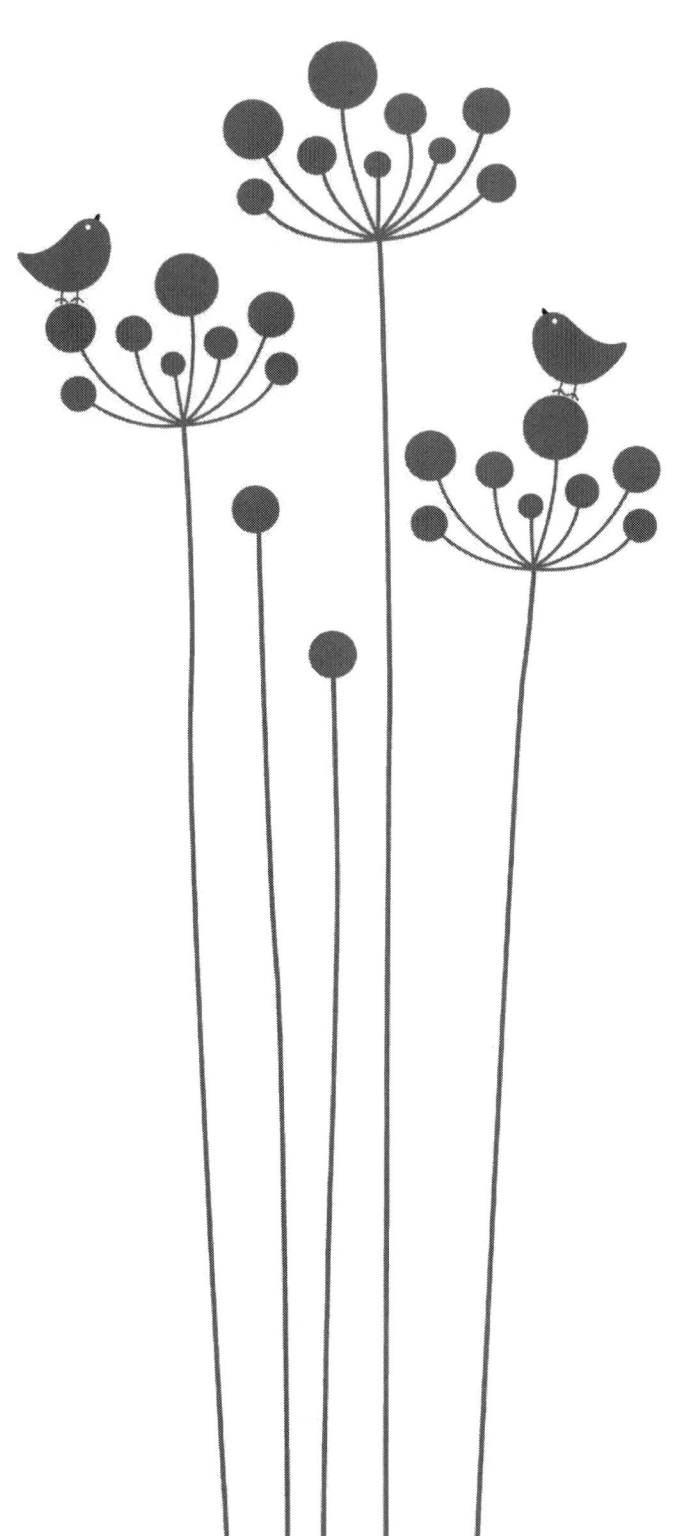

Reassurance

I need to be reassured

of your feelings for me.

I need to be reassured

of my place in our relationship.

My heart needs to be reassured,

because it is hurting.

Please communicate with me.

My mind has to stop

raging like a wild river.

Fireplace

We are happy together

just walking in the park

or along the beach,

or laying on a bear skin rug

in front of a fire place,

watching the sparks

as they pop.

That's happiness.

Fast and Faster

When we are together,

I feel all of your emotions.

I sense it as your heart

beats fast and faster.

I feel it when we touch.

I hear it when you speak.

I love you because

you are so sensitive.

Before We Met

Before we met,
I felt that something was missing.

Since we met,
that lonely spot has been filled
with your caring, your sharing,
your consideration,
and most of all,
your love.

You Are Everything

You are everything

I have ever wanted in a friend.

You are everything

I have ever wanted in a companion.

You are everything

I have ever wanted in a lover.

You are everything to me.

Here is my heart,

take care of it.

Lonely Regrets

It's not ever fun
being apart and lonely.

Loneliness sometimes brings
heart changes.

Don't allow your mind or heart
to make those mistakes.

You will regret your loneliness
in days to come.

Hanging In

I'm hanging in there

as long as required.

I'm committed to loving you.

I can't let go.

Maybe you could be

more considerate

of my feelings.

Because I do love you.

Leave My Past Behind

I'm trying to

leave my past behind.

I'm trying to

find myself.

Can you support

my struggles

as I search to

find a new future?

Moods

Many days are passing

full of unhappiness.

Let's set aside

our personal moods and angers,

and consider the importance

of our happiness and

of our relationship

in the many days to come.

Next Level

Please don't ask me

to change for you,

I cannot fulfill your request.

I can only change for myself.

Maybe, then, our relationship

can advance to the next level.

Forgiveness

Sometimes it's hard to forgive,

and some things can't be forgiven.

There is an old proverb that says:

"What you no longer see

with your eyes

will slowly disappear

in your heart."

Fine Wine

Your love is like fine wine.
Your loving is like
the best delicacy.

Without Meeting

Without meeting and
being in one another's life,
we can't smile or share
our love and feelings.

Without meeting,
our love
will always be in the dark.

Our Plans

Now, I can only live in memory

of our relationship,

of our touch,

our walk in the park,

our desire to have a family,

our plans to make

our hearts beat as one.

Pray For Change

Something has gone wrong
in our relationship.

Could we do a little searching
in our hearts
for solutions to our problems?

Let's ask for guidance
from up above.

Prayer has the power
to change everything.

Take a Minute

*Could we take a minute
to share with each other
how happy we are
that we met?*

*Today is an anniversary.
The happiest day of our lives.
The Heavenly Father must
have had a plan
for us to become as one.*

Thank you, Father.

Starlight

You have shined like a star

in my life.

Your shimmer has directed me

in how to love and

how to be loved.

Your enduring light

has made me the

person I am today.

Don't Judge

*Our relationship and our love
should not be judged
on the length of time
we have known each other,
but judged on our feelings
and the number of times
we have made each other happy.*

Share Your Life

Don't tell me that you love me.
Show me!
Don't tell me you are sorry for
hurting me.
Mend it!
Don't tell me that you want to
share your life with me.
Be there and prove it!

Trying Too Hard

I'm trying to be in control.
I'm trying to be strong.
But each time I shed a tear,
maybe I'm trying too hard,
and that makes the tears flow.

Blunder

Allow me to blunder.

Allow me to make mistakes.

Allow me to take responsibility

for my actions.

But please,

be there to catch me

should I fall.

You Are

You are a source of energy.

You are full of fun and laughter.

You make me smile when I'm sad.

You give me confidence

when I thought it impossible.

You give me the attention I need

to protect me

from the outside world.

Willing

I'm waiting for

the day

to hear you say

you are in love with me.

That will be

the day

all my dreams

will come true.

I'm willing to wait.

Cuddles and Kisses

Our love for each other
is like getting presents
each day.
We are always doing
happy things
for each other
to make our love
blossom
with warm feelings,
cuddles and kisses.

Waiting

When we are apart

for whatever the reason,

our love protects us

from being lonely.

No other can enter

our space of love.

I will always be here

waiting for your return.

Happiness

As each day passes

I try to find ways

to make you happy,

to see you smile,

to kiss your soft lips,

to hug your body,

to make love to you.

Today, Tomorrow, Forever

*Years and years ago
we gazed into
each other's eyes
as we held hands
in the park.*

*Our deep friendship
and respect
led us into forever love.*

Today, tomorrow, forever.

Enter My Heart

When you entered my life
you entered
my space,
my freedom,
my ability to think clearly.
Thank you
for entering my heart.

You have made me happy.

Don't Pretend

Don't pretend
to love me
when you don't.

Don't pretend
to love me
when you can't.

Just love me,
should your heart
tell you it's okay.

Reserved

If I have been too aggressive
in our relationship,
it's only that you
have been so reserved.

Or maybe I fear losing
the opportunity
to get to know you.

All of my reasons are true.
I just fell in love with you.

Words Aren't Easy

*Sometimes words
aren't easy for me
to tell you
that I love you,
but
I'll always be here
to enhance
your happiness.*

Let's Not Blame

Let's not blame each other
for our unhappiness.
Let's each of us search
for what it is
that makes us unhappy,
and perhaps then,
we will find happiness
within ourselves.

Apology

I apologize to you

for showing you my true feelings.

I made the mistake

of thinking I could have

a future with you.

Today, please accept my apology

for that which can never be.

Decisions

I've made many decisions,

trying to find happiness.

The best decision I've made

was to fall in love with you.

You've made me so happy.

Thank you,

you are beautiful.

Give Me The Chance

If you need to cry

when you're sad,

here are my shoulders

to lean on.

If you're happy

and want me to share

your happiness,

I will be there.

Requirements

I realize our requirements

are similar

in many ways.

Maybe we can communicate

long enough to find out

what they are,

and then we can cater

to each other's needs.

As I Grow

Allow me to make mistakes

and to be wrong.

Allow me to admit

to my wrongs

and to my mistakes.

Don't expect me to be

always right and perfect.

Allow me to be me,

as I grow.

Who I Am

You know who you are.

You have been there to help me
find my identity.

You have filled
a lonely spot in my heart.

I want to be loved by you.

Thanks to you,
now I know who I am.

Little Secrets

I promise

to love you,

to make you happy,

to share your joys,

and to listen

when you need

to share your little secrets.

Tell Me What

Tell me what you feel

about me.

Tell me if you love me.

I want to enhance

your happiness.

I will be there

whenever you need me.

To Hold You

After a hard day of work

I cannot get home fast enough

to share prime time with you.

To hold you in my arms.

To feel your soft touch.

To love you.

Without You

*I have planned my life
around you.*

You are my happiness.

*Without you,
I have nothing.*

Together We Stand

*I've searched all my life for
someone to love,
someone to accept me for me,
someone I could share
my little secrets with,
someone to catch me,
should I fall.*

Wonderful Touch

Every time I close my eyes to sleep

I see your pretty smile.

I feel your soft and wonderful touch.

I pray never to wake.

Just let me sleep.

Wrong

If loving you is wrong,

don't try to correct me.

I really don't want to be right.

Let me continue to be wrong.

I don't care if I'm wrong.

Discover

Discover what love is.

Discover our feelings

for each other.

Discover how to share,

and to communicate.

Understand who we are

as we discover love.

Whatever Reason

It's okay
for whatever reason
you have for loving me.

I'm happy now,
more than I've ever been.

Please love me forever.

Our Future

I've admired you all of our lives,
because of the friendship
we've shared.

Now I'm ready and willing
to make a lifetime commitment
to you and to our future
as a family.

Please think of our happiness.

Let Us

Let us pray together.
Let us pray to whomever we serve.
Let us give thanks for our blessings,
to whomever we serve.
Let us ask for blessings to continue
being strong in our relationship.
Let us give thanks,
to whomever we serve,
for the blessings received.

Classy

I can never forget

your pretty face,

your beautiful smile,

your classic walk, and

your pleasing personality.

Those qualities make you

who you are.

You are beautiful.

Lovely Thoughts

I enjoy the energy

you put into our relationship.

It reassures me

of how much you love me.

I treasure you

for all of your lovely thoughts.

You really make me happy.

One Smile For Me

I smile
when no one sees me.
I smile
because I'm happy
with you in my thoughts.
I smile
knowing that only you
bring total happiness to my heart.

Easy Now

It's easy for me now
to express myself,
my desires,
where I want my life
to go from here.
I have found a solution
to my loneliness.
Love.
Thank you for loving me
and for showing me
other ways to be happy.

Sad Tears

I have seen you sad,

with tears in your eyes

many times

in our relationship.

I never took the time

to realize how often

you were saddened.

I apologize

for not recognizing

your unhappiness.

Loving You

Loving you
has been the best thing
that has happened to me.

My wishes and dreams
were fulfilled
when I met you.

Now, we can be happy
together.

My Time

Allow me time
to express myself
about how I really feel.

Allow me to cry,
when it's necessary
for my cleansing.

Allow me to express myself,
if only in my space
of loneliness.

Then – we can communicate.

Deserted Island

If I were stranded

on a deserted island

with no help in sight

and one wish

before I was found,

that wish would be to be

rescued by you.

Stop and Listen

Stop and listen,
before
you voice an opinion.

Listen to someone
who knows
about love,
courtship,
marriage,
and most of all,
honesty.

Always There

Day after day
you show me
how much
you love me,
and how much
you care.

Please allow me
the chance to share,
and to show you
that
I will always be there.

Miracles

I believe in miracles.
I know it in my mind.
I feel it when we touch.
I see it in your smile.

Thanks to the Heavenly Father
for making you my miracle.

I'll Be There

I'll be there
when you need to cry.

I'll be there
when you are sad.

I'll be there
to hold you,
and to assure you
that
I'll always be there.

Second Time Around

I admit to not being
considerate enough
to your feelings,
your thoughts.

I admit hurting you and
breaking your heart.
That's my fault.

Those were the growing up years.
Allow me to make mistakes,
and to heal the wounds,
the second time around.

Easy to Say

*It's easy to tell you
that I love you,
but hard to say
goodbye.*

*Perhaps we shouldn't
say goodbye,
because
that would make us sad.*

Forgiving Mistakes

I've made mistakes
in my life.
I'm sorry for choices
I've made.
I realize
some of my mistakes
can't be forgiven,
and some
can't be forgotten.

By Grace,
I can forgive myself.

I Can't Love You

I can feel.

I can touch.

But I can't love you.

You must know this

before we make love.

I trust you will do

the things you can live with.

I'm sorry.

I can't love you.

Your Shadow

I never knew what love was
before you came into
my thoughts.

Your shadow has changed
my concept of
caring,
feeling,
and sharing.

Thank you for my new image.

If I Choose

*I can only change
if I choose to.*

*I change
because it's my choice.*

*I do love you
and want to make you happy.*

Let it be my choice.

I Saw Her First

I watched her walk away while
I was seated at the lunch table.
She made my stomach bubble inside.
She switched from side to side
as she walked.
I couldn't wait.
I had to find a way to meet her.
Minutes later, she came to my table
and asked if she could join me.
I started to stutter,
spitting out 'yes'.
Today she is my wife.
The love of my life.

Follow us at:

www.lamblambertauthor.com

www.instagram.com/lamblamberttheauthor

Contact us:

info@lamblambertauthor.com

lambtheauthor@gmail.com

Affairs of the Heart, Vol. 1

Available on Amazon.com!

288 COLOR illustrated

free verse selections

5  reviews

Kaitlyn C on December 8, 2016

This is such a beautiful book! I couldn't put it down. It would make a great gift for that person who has everything. It is so heartfelt and genuine. I have a copy for myself and one for my son. I can't wait to read his next book due out in the spring. This is a book I will turn to again and again. I will use it when I need comfort, when I need something special to pass on to a friend and when I just need a reminder that there is still love in the world.

****

Love expressed and wrapped in a gorgeous package
By Pieslak on December 2, 2016

This incredibly beautiful book would make the ideal Valentine's present. My brother bought a copy from the author and I had the joy of being able to read it. Kudos to the designer and congrats on the author's first book. A prize winner with heart warming sentiment.

****

This book is really two wonderful books. It is powerful free verse poetry that ...
By Amazon Customer on December 7, 2016

This book is really two wonderful books. It is powerful free verse poetry that says beautifully what we all have thought, and it is also a book of art so lovely that you do not need the words.

****

Every verse was my favorite.
By Kindle Customer on December 9, 2016

Beautifully written. Every time I thought I found my favorite verse, I would find another! I cannot wait for his next book

****

By patti on December 12, 2016
This book is truly a work of art straight from the heart. The experiences of love, joy, pain, loss, faith and so much more, have been beautifully put into words by Harlen "Lamb" Lambert. And the artwork that accompanies those words is stunning. Amazing job, Harlen and Sharron! I look forward to the next volume.

COMING SOON.....

BADGE OF COLOR
Breaking the Silence
A Memoir

From southern states cotton fields to California police officer; from Jim Crow South to John Birch Society, Orange County, CA.

This is the true story about the first black police officer hired for the Santa Ana Police Department in 1966. Hailed a hero, rejected by his peers, profound hatred, bigotry, and arrogance of powers would drive his career and life.

Made in the USA
San Bernardino, CA
24 February 2020